ALSO BY WALTER BENTON

NEVER A GREATER NEED

THIS IS A BORZOI BOOK

PUBLISHED IN NEW YORK

BY ALFRED A. KNOPF

THIS IS
MY BELOVED

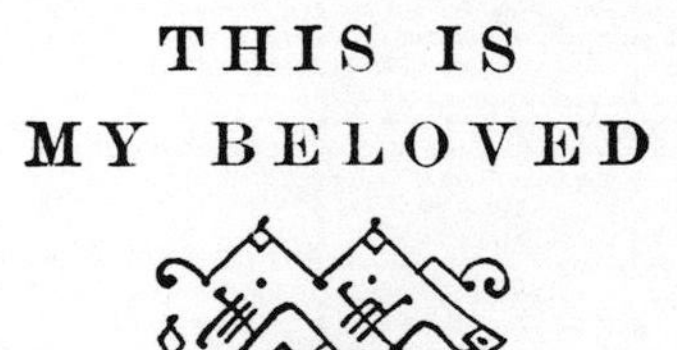

THIS IS MY BELOVED

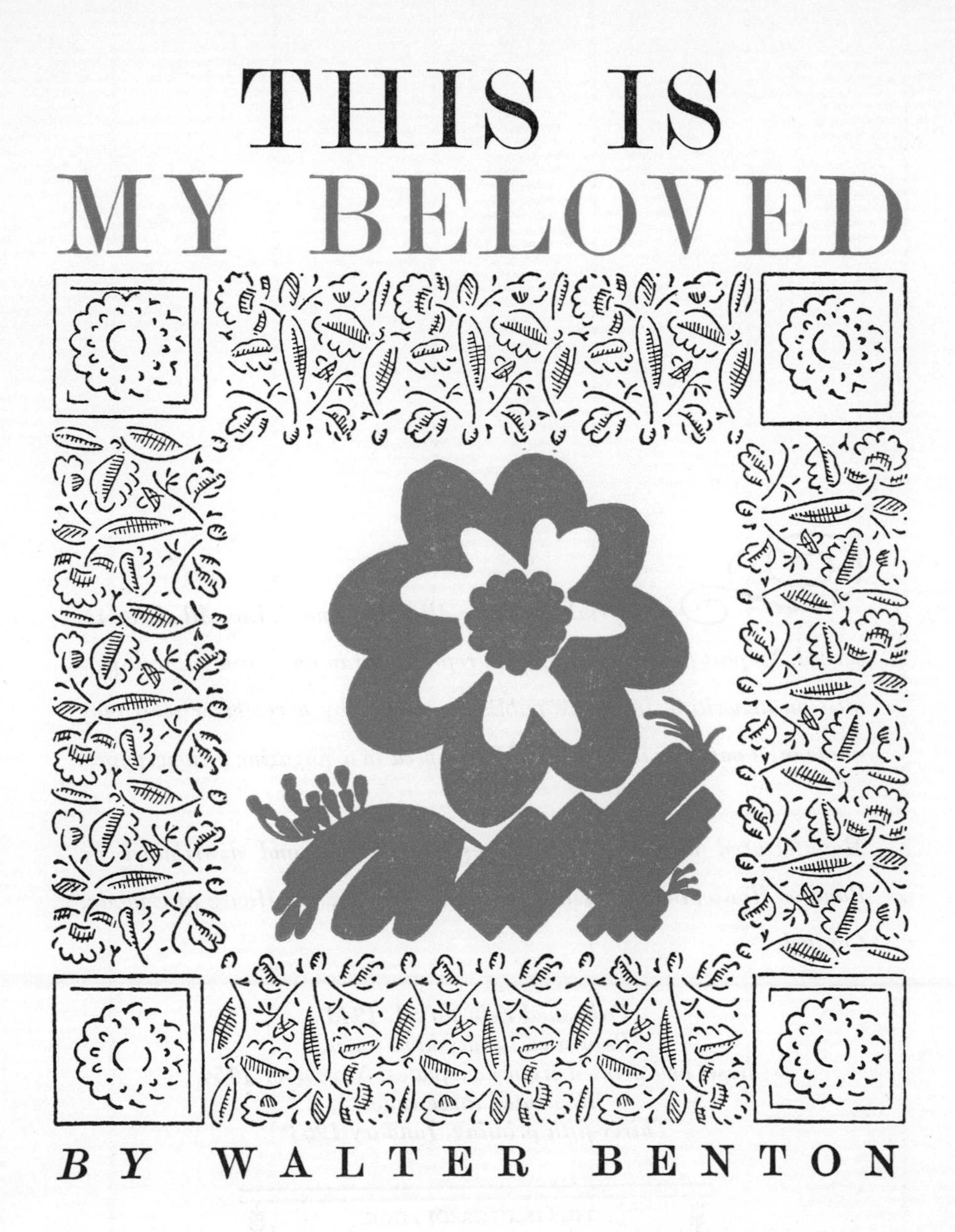

BY WALTER BENTON

ALFRED A. KNOPF *NEW YORK*
1963

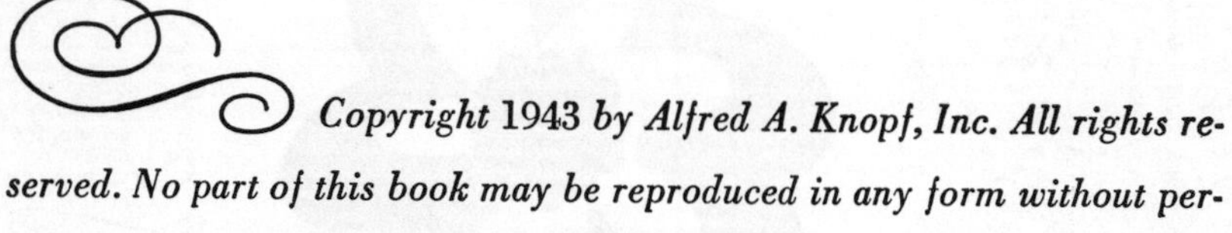

Manufactured in the United States of America and distributed by Random House, Inc. Published in Canada by Random House of Canada, Limited.

Published February 1, 1943
Reprinted twenty-nine times
Reset and printed from new plates, November 1954
Reprinted three times
Thirty-fifth printing, January 1963

THIS IS A BORZOI BOOK,
PUBLISHED BY ALFRED A. KNOPF, INC.

for Lillian

I

Entry *April 28*

Because hate is legislated . . . written into
the primer and the testament,
shot into our blood and brain like vaccine or vitamins

Because our day is of time, of hours — and the clock-hand turns,
closes the circle upon us: and black timeless night
sucks us in like quicksand, receives us totally —
without a raincheck or a parachute, a key to heaven or the last long look

I need love more than ever now . . . I need your love,
I need love more than hope or money, wisdom or a drink

Because slow negative death withers the world — and only yes
can turn the tide
Because love has your face and body . . . and your hands are tender
and your mouth is sweet — and God has made no other eyes like yours.

ENTRY *May 4*

You rise out of sleep like a growing thing rises
out of the garden soil.
Two leaves part to be your mouth, two tender seedleaves —
and your eyes are wonderfully starlike,
your eyes are luminous and soft as the velvet of pansies.

Darling, good morning.

Our arms are empty of each other for a moment only.
How beautifully you turn . . . your mouth tilts to let my kisses in.
Lie still . . . we shall be longer.

We need so little room, we two . . . thus on a single pillow —
as we move nearer,
nearer heaven — until I burst inside you like a screaming rocket.

Then we are quietly apart . . . returning to this earth.

Entry *May 11*

Some see you in similes: Helen's rich curves,
colors autumn has. You please them
as an opium dream pleases, or you smile like the sun is rising —

or you walk proudly like a woman courted.
But I see you best unrelated . . . with not a metaphor to your name:
your hair not like the silk of corn or spiders but like your hair,
your mouth resembling nothing so wonderfully much as your own mouth.

Why should I say you are like a slender water bird on wing?
This is but a slide of you, a fraction. Or that your thighs are lilies —
lilies are cold,
lilies are neither quick nor scented . . . they do not stain the night
with velvet musk — they cannot fire love and quench it.

I mean . . . compliments become you
as tinsel becomes a tall snow covered cedar in a mountain cedar wood.

Entry *May 18*

Your words are born, not spoken.
Dimensional, soft-vowelled words, palpable to the eye or to the fingertip:
exquisitely curved, as the young that flowers conceive.

Often have I watched your lips shape words . . . and your tongue
nudge them out like small birds not wholly certain of their wings.
Your sweetest words
are those shaped ovally, like plums or wild birds' eggs.

And the long bright ribbons you laugh —
the multitudes of hyacinth and bluebells.

When I see words like soft grey catkins I know they are of love —
whatever else my ears register.
And because your mouth is like the flesh of ripe fig, often I take

your words unsaid . . . as the brown honey-bear slips his red tongue
into the nest of sleeping bees to take out honey.
And the sweet, natural taste,
the pussy-willow feel of your words is lovelier than their shape or music.

ENTRY *May 25*

All right, sulk. But as you sit, so . . . knees high—
the wild, spiral feathers accentuating the meeting of your thighs,
like dark grass grown in too rich a soil —
you are beautifully eloquent.

Or when your gown loosens,
falls off the small fierce faces of your breasts, as the cowl falls off
the face of a hunter's falcon . . . I attend, nerve-naked.

I memorize you . . . walking as if to music. Your dress lies
against the cheeks and hollow of your thighs like running water.
Your breasts nod yes each step,
your slow involute hips cradle the eternal synonym for God.

The dress censors not a syllable of you.
Articulate eyes wink from your breasts and belly, signal from your throat —
beckon from your knees, your waist . . . your mobile shoulders.

Yes, your body makes eyes at me from every salient,
promises warm, lavish promises —
curved, colored . . . finished in warm velvet, like baby rabbits.

Entry *June 3*

Your eyes never opened after the last kiss.

We had loved hard —

it's all over your throat and hair, it lies on your mouth like a wild

red flower: it's on your cheeks and forehead in waning radiance.

The wonderful strength of your thighs is back to gentle beauty.

Your nipples contract . . . gather in like blossoms for the night.

Your hand half-sleeping finds me . . . your touch is very dear.

Now you are all sleep, alone with yourself — and a tall blue fence

around you: not a tendon taut, not a secret secret,

you are all sleep and alone in a warm and velvet world —

many an idle dream is looking for a home of sleep like yours to happen in.

ENTRY *June 11*

Why am I looking at you like this?

Only because I want to remember this,

all this . . . the musty glasses and the checkered tablecloth,

cigarette butts, burnt matches, spilled beer and crumpled napkins.

The juke box — and the sailor with his hand inside the girl's dress.

The strong urine smell —

and the whores and the fairies watching like spiders.

And the way the fingered piano eggs the dancers on to exaggerate

their coupling gestures. The recorded orgasm of the saxophone —

Hey, bartender . . . isn't it about time we had one on the house?

Darling . . . oh, I want to remember you always, everywhere —

in a tavern or in church, asleep or taking bath . . . I must not ever

forget the look in your eyes

when you had drunk and wanted to hurry home and be loved to sleep.

ENTRY *June 12*

Sleep late, nobody cares what time it is.
Sunday morning, coffee in bed . . . then love
with coffee flavored kisses. And your tongue dripping honey like a ripe fig.

I have been hours awake looking at you lithely at rest in the free
natural way rivers bed and clouds shape.
Your bedgown gathers up your full round thighs, rolls over your hips.
Your breasts are snub like children's faces . . . and your navel deep

as a god's eye.
Yes, your lips match your teats beautifully, rose and rose.
The hair of your arm's hollow and where your thighs meet
agree completely, being brown and soft to look at like a nest of field mice.
Praise be the walls that shelter you from eyes that are not mine!

Love, not prayers, shall be our offering this day.
We shall praise God with absolute embraces . . . our bodies shall sing Him
in His own incomparable tongue.
Prayer is humbleness, I cannot be humble with the wealth of you beside me.

ENTRY *June 17*

Somewhere cities crouch . . . cower —

(Move nearer me)

The violet sky parasols us, and from the incandescent noon

the sun pours into the moist, open earth.

The woods are sweet and bedwarm as your breasts in the morning.

Somewhere a clock is timing us —

hurry . . . with the grass still under us and the sun kissing us pink

with lover's lips, not scavenger's teeth . . . come, love me.

You smile yes . . . and your lips part, fill out like leeches.

Yes is a darting hummingbird inside your throat — and in your armpits yes

is sweeter than the ground mint staining your warm, naked thighs.

Your breasts are wonderfully alive under my kisses.

Tremble against me —

if we must spill blood, let it flow thickly like yellow honey on a tongue,

let it meet as in a flower . . . and the petals close upon it —

yes, let it live . . . timecapsuled in a new generation of you and me.

Entry *June 22*

Were I Pygmalion or God

I would make you exactly as you are . . . in all dimensions.

From your warm hair to your intimate toes would you be

wholly in your own image. I would change nothing, add or take away.

The same full red flower would model for your mouth —

and from the same seashore

would I bring the small translucent earshapes of your ears.

O the lovely throat that I could duplicate!

The tender arms!

I would shape your breasts the shape of the hungry little faces

they are now . . . and tip them with the same quick mouths.

I could not make your eyes deeper than they are —

nor softer to look into . . . nor could I turn your hips, your thighs,

your belly in a sweeter curve: nor indent the hollows

of your loins more tenderly — or store more honey there or fire.

How would I name you . . . need you ask? You know. By the scarlet

and the blue you wear when love is upon you, by the yellow

tongues — by the warm white fragrance . . . by the slender leaves.

ENTRY *June 24*

Last night we entered our bed through opposite doors.

Hours we lay awake, entrenched . . . before the trapdoor gave

and we were hurtling down in jerky sleep.

When we suddenly awoke, our bodies were together in the warm bed lap —

and I was taking deep swollen kisses out of your brimming mouth.

Your lips cushioned the inherent murder in your teeth.

My body grew to fit your body —

and the opened blossoms of you were flaming, full . . . and making honey.

There in the jungle twilight, stark naked god slipped in between us

and the lightning struck —

and in the light I saw you, you were lovelier by many years than yesterday.

Today . . . your mind moved back into your face, willing away

your last night's beauty.

And the hard mask of resolution lies dull upon you like a bad make-up.

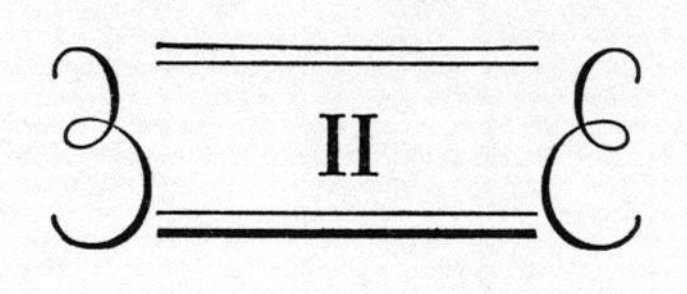
II

ENTRY *June 27*

I stood long where you left me.

Night was all around me

and the stars pecked at it with fierce acetylene silver beaks.

A little thin moon scarred the sky.

Then I walked . . . my arm around the emptiness of you beside me.

And because you were total in my eyes like sudden blindness,

I saw only you.

You were my purpose and my way,

you were the bright articulate lights and the dark lonely streets,

you were each door and window . . . and every passing face.

And because you were indelible in my blood and brain

in infinite copies — without drink or delirium

my mind conceived you . . . my senses registered you dimensionally.

And it was beautiful . . . O then it was beautiful

in a high beautiful city . . . in a tall lighted beautiful world —

the moon was young and the stars winked like fireflies in tall grass:

night was a jewelled tent around us

and we were wonderfully alone and sleepy as we always are just after love.

Entry *July 26*

The thin, skeletal moon reminded me . . . and the sharp
electric stars, when I walked to meet you.
And meeting you, your face — grim and implacable — reminded me.

And the studied way you controlled pleasure, even when we had drunk —
danced, heard swing music: even when you read my new poem to you.
All these reminded me. A month had passed —
a month, by the gaunt red moon like the mark of an incandescent thumbnail

Your mind's cosmetic lay frightfully upon you; muddied your eyes
and settled on your mouth. Entered your skin like acid.
How will you be when you have fully torn the rainbows off my eyes?

Ah, we will be poor then, you and I — sorry and wrong, alone and poor —
for all our righteousness and love we may have found in others.
Yes, I will be poor . . . what else not having you can mean to me?

And as for you — all the things you cannot ever be, you are
only because my love is like the magic touch of stars. You wear my love,
and all who see you say: how beautifully his love becomes her!

1

Entry *August 9*

Each season of each year I will be forgetting you
all over. Each season, every year.
I will need to forget you each summer, spring . . . autumn and winter.

Each summer I will be forgetting: you forever naked, you brown with the sun's
fire, you moving in massive adagio like a seal turning in water.
You lying in the sun — or looking darling
in a cotton dress. You — and the kites. Connecticut . . . and you.

Autumn, I will be forgetting meeting you,
and the first long kiss on the green bedlam hill, under the rash of stars —
I could not leave your mouth . . . remember? And the garret rooms
we lived in. The bittersweet we gathered and the rich red sumac in the high
hectic woods where the air was ripe apples and the colors chrysanthemum.

Each winter there will be long evenings together to forget, reading or talking —
having friends. Greenup on the Ohio.
The sweetness of you in bed . . . and growing sleepy in each other's arms.
And you returning to me each morning "for one minute only"
nakedly, for warmth — your mouth full of cool mint toothpaste kisses.

Spring will be the hardest to forget, with lovers everywhere —
O spring will be hard . . . forgetting the early violets along the Hocking,
hitching to Marietta — and the lamb that broke the fold to follow us.
Love we made beside the river, lying on the grass . . . how beautiful you
were —

pale-green where you showed naked to the moon,
your eyes were tearbright, your eyes were full of moonlight and of stars
and you were wonderfully warm and trembling when you let me in.

2

I will be forgetting you each day and every hour.
Each night and day, each hour something
wonderful and dear of you will ring my heart and knock upon my mind.

Each time I hear Gilbert and Sullivan — or Strauss, see ginkgo trees,
read Lewis Carroll: see flowering dogwood or smell
locust, acacia, sweet honeysuckle, lily of the valley, or wild roses.

I shall forever be forgetting the quick happy kisses, like samples —
when my own lips could never fully capture yours.
And the deep ravenous kisses when I awoke wanting you at night.

Sunday will be the hardest to forget, late Sunday mornings,
with your sleep-rich body . . . and your hardly opened eyes terribly tender.
The articulate wordlessness of your lips and tongue —
and the natural way you raised your gown and fitted yourself to me.
O I drew love like honey-steeped wine from every mouth of you —
and when we had loved our fill, we laughed, and we were very hungry.
Then we ate fruit with cream and sugar, bacon — sausages and cakes
with rich brown maple syrup . . . and drank strong, fragrant coffee.

3

Each time I know beauty, it shall be through you.
When joy lifts me high . . . or sorrow breaks me —
when I love again, my senses conditioned to you will be forgetting you

anew. Each kiss that fills my mouth shall fill it with your lips —
yes, each time my eyelids crumble and close
under blood's fired impact, when love strikes home — yours will be the mouth

and yours the disengaging arms —
your heart it will be leaping in your throat and beating in your thighs.
Your relieved breasts. Your simmering loins. Your soft happy eyes.

I will be forgetting you in silence and in song . . . in silence will I
dream dreams of you too wonderful to dare aloud —
and of words I shall not use for anyone but you I shall make poems.

When a star falls, I shall wish for you.
When the moon is new, I shall wish for you.
When a bird looks into my window, when a leaf falls before me, when I find
a fern in flower — I shall wish for you.

And when autumn lays out her lavish colors . . . her warm brown,
ripe yellow, her exciting red all over the hills and fields,
like a lovely woman undressing — I shall look for you.

ENTRY *August 22*

As the world gathers momentum toward nihilation
on all fronts — we walk apart,
each to his own lonely end . . . not hand in hand as lovers walk.

Yet I would enter time's infinite pages more happily with you
than in the company of Christs and Dantes — comets and constellations!

Darling . . . before the distance widens beyond reach and sight —
look this way, give me your hand — that the stars may say of us:

The last we saw of them was when they kissed,
then beautifully naked walked as if into a sea of bright blue water —
leaving their bodies like old clothes upon the shore.

ENTRY *August 27*

The white full moon like a great beautiful whore
solicits over the city, eggs the lovers on —
the haves . . . walking in twos to their beds and to their mating.

I walk alone. Slowly. No hurry. Nobody's waiting.
My love who loved me (she said) is gone. My love is gone.

And I walk alone. It's goodnight time . . . the haves are everywhere,
in parked cars and passing taxis —
the still, abstracted figures pressed against walls and niched
in dark doorways . . . each two arm-hooped into one body rigid with joy.

A lighted window holds me like high voltage. I see . . .
cupped in the bed's white palm, the haves — O she is beautiful, her breasts
are white dogwood and her thighs
barked poplars growing out of the dark-matted jungle of her crotch.

He is kissing her, interminably her mouth . . . and one by one each breast
is carried to the lips with tender violence.
Now he lays his hand to her secret body. Her frantic thighs invite
invasion. He covers her, enters . . . turns god — and my eyelids fall.

Entry *August 29*

It was like something done in fever, when nothing fits,
mind into mind nor body into body . . . when nothing
meets or equals — when dimensions lie and perceptions go haywire.

With what an alien sense my fingers curved about her breasts
and searched the tangled dark where love lay hiding!
I closed my eyes better to imagine you —
but the rehearsed body would not ratify the mind's deception.

The kisses of her mouth, the rhythm natural to love — and the exciting
musk with which love haloes itself . . . these thwarted my imagination.
Her love, too, was centered and intent,

it did not reach her eyes and forehead, or light her throat
as your love did —
it did not fill the room . . . or spread all over the ceiling of the sky.
It did not span the years and miles and hold hands with beast and God.

Nor did her thighs rise with that splendid grade I stroked from memory.
Her body met me unlike your body
and I entered the heaven of her uneasily . . . and could not stay —
for my heart being yours released no blood to make ready for love.

Entry *September 6*

I saw autumn today . . . incipiently, on the sunset
and the leaf — in the spontaneous whitecaps shingling the bay
and the window-displayed chrysanthemums and asters.
I saw its night's water color leavings on the cottonwood and the maple —
and heard its voice
in the locust's high powered chatter in the camouflaged somewhere.

Ah! Fierce exhilaration flows through me like dry current.
Soon we shall walk on the sunny side of the street . . . hold hands,
mingle in bed for warmth. Autumn is our season — yours and mine.

See, I have lain naked and long in the sun to match your body.
We shall look beautiful lying side by side.
The stain of the season is rich upon you, only your breasts are white
as the winter grouse . . . you have not shown them to the sun —
nor the low of your belly where you are white, soft and dark-feathered.

Entry *September 12*

When all the poems on the theme have been written

and all the night and day dreams dreamt, without prophecy or fulfilment.

When hope sustains us no longer —

nor being drunk or busy or therapeutically in love keeps us from remembering.

When our new interests, our richer lives . . . require quotes

to qualify their meanings: and however hard we try,

we can exploit our grievances no further to fortify our resolutions —

what will we do to keep madness sulking in the brain?

When we have forgotten even why we parted, if we ever knew it at all —

remembering, however, when we could sleep naked and be warm together,

kiss, though with a cold —

when even baby-talk became you . . . yes,

and everything I said was sweet or funny and everything you did was beautiful.

Entry *September 17*

See, I alter nothing. This is you and I in dark-gray lead,
on plain white paper. No flattering
magenta colors. No accompaniment in minor key — or brilliant arpeggios.

Just sit as you are, or stand . . . and do whatever you are doing, while
the kodak shutter winks you into permanence.
Just turn the last flight of stairway as I open the door — and say hello.

Just slip into your nightdress, stumble into bed,
say goodnight . . . and go soft all over. Turn, drape yourself over me
like a lissom python, our smooth bodies touching everywhere.
Sleep rising from you lulls me like the sweet smoke of hashish.

Leave everything exactly as it is: the undone hair clouding the pillow
and the small ears lost snugly somewhere in the clouds. The little
blue veins under your breasts and the brown birth marks inside your thighs.
The bittersweet climbing the beech
and the partridge berry trailing on the ground.
The early crocuses and the second-flowering hawthorn.

You see, this needs no retouching. The colors are natural and the shape
universal. Therefore
I shall never forget you . . . nor will your memory be ever free of me.
For your arms are my home — and my arms the circle you cannot leave, however far you go.

ENTRY *September 27*

How dark is the river! How still . . . and dark
with deep, slow moving darkness!
the seagulls, dreaming violence, cried me awake with their strangely anguished
voices — like the voices of women being taken in love.

Here where nights are deep as clear deep water, and the sky spawns stars
abundantly . . . teeming with golden inflorescence:
away from the world we lived in — the streets we walked together and the roofs
we flew the kites from. The doors we entered and the bed we loved on.

Far from the late sunny autumns . . . the walks under the McGuffy Elms
and the coffeeshop where we played truant, convocation hours —
I watch the season go — with you,
the summer close, and the year's end draw nearer, and the world's . . .

Hear the crows heckle the straw-man in the cornpatch across the river?
It is so strange, this my need of you.
Yesterday I gathered seashells
at Compo Beach, but I had no one to show them to. And when I saw blue heron
fishing in the Saugatuck shallows — I cried to Cora: " Lillian, look! "

ENTRY *October 15*

Everyone is sleeping. Nothing wakes. The woods
are motionless. The wind is down to a whisper.
Sleep hums like current — yes, audibly — through the bright steel night.

The evening star rises like a flaming wick.
Hills fit into hills like lovers, their great dark straddling thighs
clasping still greater darkness where they meet. A star breaks,
arcs down the night — like God striking a match across the cathedral ceiling.

Therefore I wish: see my lips move — making your name. It is so still,
so still. I am sure that you must hear me —

ENTRY *October 17*

This is how the sun rose over Paine Mountain:
the high horizon paled, inching upwards
like a stripteaser lifting her dress to show her white body.
Cloud-fragments pinkened like nipples, and the icy ledges refracted
the white . . . raying out like the Resurrection.

The height of the mountain later, appeared the sun.

And this is how it set:
all day it slunk along about a witch's height
when suddenly (it must have stumbled)
it dropped out of sight somewhere in Northfield Hills, where the Mad
River is. And the lit clouds fanned out in tall fantastic branches of plum
and apple heavy with blossom, and the sky was sea-green behind them.

Then I remembered . . . you loved apple blossoms — and I reached out
over the dun, amber hills
and broke off large sprays, abundant with sweet air and soft colors.
I shall give them to you some spring . . . when our love comes home.

ENTRY *October 24*

The Green Hills sprawl in the last sun of autumn.
This morning I lay on a hillside
and the sun was warm . . . it was like lying naked under your naked kisses —

and eleven years of you moved through my memory — eleven years
walked, laughed, lay, loved me . . . ate, drank, quarrelled, made up.
The sweat of the leaves under my feet excited me — leaves left where they fall
are sweeter in the air than crushed green mint or fallen apples.

O what is this that drives me so as if to keep some destined date!

The sun lowers. I smoke hard to check the jitters.
The train drives a shrieking wedge between the hills. I close my eyes,
I move to give you the window seat beside me —
though two states lie between us . . . and four long terrible months.

III

Entry *October 26*

My heart swells . . . bulges —

my heart presses against my lungs, I cannot breathe, it rises to my throat

and throttles my words —

O it will burst sky-high surely and a cloud of starlings will fly out!

A swarm of luminous moths . . . and boisterous starlings!

Why do they stare at me as I stride the Village streets,

crossing the crossings against the lights and recognizing no one?

Are my eyes too bright? Is my head too high?

Or does it really show, that kiss — does it sit on my lips like a moth

on a leaf, has your kiss blossomed on my mouth into a scarlet flower?

Entry *October 31*

How long . . . how long can I live this night!

Look . . . the clouds shine —

darling, how did you do it? The wind is soft, the rain is beautiful —

what did you do to the wind, and the rain, and the clouds?

And to me?

See, I am drunk, high . . . I am drunk on you as on a reefer!

We will cross here where the street is crowded that I may hold your hand

We will ride the subways that we may sit touching — that there be

no distance between us. Speak . . . that I may fill my ears with you.

Stay near me, so . . . that I may fill my lungs with you.

Come home with me . . . that I may fill my arms with you.

Come where only I can see you, and undo your dress about your throat.

And my lips will make the nipples of your breasts burst open

like acorns planted in warm spring soil. Come home with me . . .

lift your dress high — your thighs will light my room with moonlight,

and the hair in the pocket of them will recall to me

the darkness of firs and larches in the dark mountain passes.

If only I could fit my life's time into these hours — that I might say:

" I was with her from eight to twelve o'clock . . . and years passed "!

ENTRY *November 12*

I waited years today . . . one year for every hour,
all day — though I knew you could not come till night
I waited . . . and nothing else in this God's hell meant anything.

I had everything you love — shellfish and saltsticks . . . watercress,
black olives. Wine (for the watch I pawned), real cream
for our coffee. Smoked cheese, currants in port, preserved wild cherries.

I bought purple asters from a pushcart florist and placed them where
they would be between us —
imagining your lovely face among them . . .

But you did not come . . . you did not come.
You did not come. And I left the table lit and your glass filled —
and my glass empty . . . and I went into the night, looking for you.

The glittering pile, Manhattan, swarmed like an uncovered dung heap.
Along the waterfront
manlike shapes all shoulders and collar walked stiffly like shadow figures.

Later, the half-moon rose.
Everywhere the windows falling dark.
By St. Mark's church, under the iron fence, a girl was crying. And the old
steeple was mouldy with moonlight, and I was tired . . . and very lonely.

IV

ENTRY *November 15*

I knew your eyes by heart after the very first reading.
I could repeat them in detail,
remembering their elements in pearls and moonstones —
in the dark wing of a starling . . . and the bright morning faces of asters.

I learned your hair many ways . . . by the musk and visually,
by the Braille touch. I could tell which part of your body grew it:
the underhair fringing your face was sensitive like thin smoke in a draught,
between your thighs it was natural and crisp like the hearts of lettuce.

After one fitting only I could cup my hands just so —
as if they held your face.
Blindfolded, I could kiss a thousand mouths and know your lips.
I could tell time by your mouth's kisses, feel rich red colors —
taste sun-ripe fruits . . . and know the seasons of the year.

I took your body like a glass of sweet milk at bedtime.
And my eyelids let go at the hinges when I entered you. You were all I
and all of me was you — my senses rhymed with your senses
and our bodies made music and gave light . . . as all things absolute.

What is it that happened?
Now that you are gone (and why) I feel I never knew you —
though you fill me with terrible wonder . . . like the onset of madness.

Entry *November 19*

What enslaving cocktail have I sucked
from your full mouth . . . to leave me so totally yours!

The red pulp of your kisses is sweet on my tongue as the red
ripe melon meat — yes, even now,
though remembered only . . . though you are marketing your love.

I have looked too long upon you, too long . . .
and with so much love that strangers can see you in my face —
as the sun and vivid colors leave an after-image in the eyes.

Entry *November 25*

There are no stars tonight to get my bearing by.
What time is it? What season? What year?
The sky sags . . . bellies. The city gargles dust in the streets.

I am lost on an island somewhere between two rivers.
Blind buildings are all around me —
and the earth is covered with flat stones. And over me, the low
dark roof — the harbor's lifted morass and the belchings of many chimneys.

Born in Austria of Russian parents, Walter Benton has lived most of his life in the United States. After working on a farm, in a steel mill, as a window washer, as a salesman, and at various other jobs, he entered Ohio University in 1931, and in due course was graduated. He then spent five years as a social investigator in New York. During the second World War he served in the United States Army, being commissioned a lieutenant of the Signal Corps in the autumn of 1942 and later being promoted to a captaincy. He has now returned to New York, where he is devoting his time to writing. Never a Greater Need, *a selection of the best poems he has written since the publication of* This is My Beloved *in 1943, was issued in 1948.*

This book was set on the Linotype in Bodoni Book, *a printing-type so called after Giambattista Bodoni, a celebrated printer and type designer of Rome and Parma* (1740–1813). Bodoni Book *as produced by the Linotype company is not a copy of any one of Bodoni's fonts, but is a composite, modern version of the Bodoni manner. Bodoni's innovations in printing-type style were a greater degree of contrast in the " thick and thin " elements of the letters, and a sharper and more angular finish of details.*

This book was composed, printed, and bound by H. Wolff. Typographic and binding design is by W. A. Dwiggins.